Know Your

Know Your Helicopters

Thomas Hargreave

Old Pond
PUBLISHING

First published 2016

Published by
Old Pond Publishing,
An imprint of 5M Publishing Ltd,
Benchmark House,
8 Smithy Wood Drive,
Sheffield, S35 1QN, UK
Tel: +44 (0) 114 246 4799
www.oldpond.com

A catalogue record for this book is available from the British Library

ISBN 978-1-910456-54-5

Book layout by Servis Filmsetting Ltd, Stockport, Cheshire
Printed by Replika Press Pvt. Ltd.
Photos by Thomas Hargreave unless otherwise indicated

Contents

Introduction

Like any right thinking person I was always fascinated by helicopters – these unlikely-looking machines that can move in any direction and even hover whilst thumping the air into submission. There was also the mystique which surrounded the pilots and the apparently Zen-like skill required to coax one of these machines off the ground. I would later learn there was no 'Zen', just long hours of training and concentration required. I also learnt that coaxing the thing back onto the ground mattered a great deal more than getting it off the ground. Flying one of these machines was always beyond my life's ambitions until I joined the Territorial Army as a 16-year-old soldier. Whilst sweating my way up a hill on Otterburn Training Area, pondering the wisdom of my choice to be a soldier, I noticed a Gazelle helicopter parked on a small knoll on the side of the impossibly steep hill I was trying to climb, its canopy glinting in the sunshine. More importantly, beside this splendid machine, reclined in the grass, sunglasses on, apparently snoozing were two Army Air Corps pilots. I think this sort of event is referred to as a light bulb moment! Years later, I found myself in a Gazelle hovering solo for the first time; this remains the most memorable and extraordinary moment in my career. I have been lucky enough to fly some amazing machines since and have been involved in significant military events but I can assure you that the freedom of taking off and sitting in a 5 foot hover remains the most magical part of flying.

The prompt for writing this book came to me whilst leafing through some essential reading, '*Know Your Tractors*' and it occurred to me that there was a gap in the 'Know Your' series that I was well-placed to fill. I have selected helicopters which are all still very much in service and ones you are likely to see around the world rather than historic machines. If you think some are missing, do please let me know.

I hope that this book informs you and possibly inspires you to become a helicopter pilot too!

Acknowledgements

This book would not have been possible without the generous support of:

'Q' and Juliette Smith
Captain Dave Wilson MBE
Major Jamie Lavalley
Lieutenant Colonel 'JP' Peters
Brian Nichols
Major Toby Jarvis
Philip Amadeus

HQ Aviation
Police Air Services Scotland
US Army
UK Army Air Corps
Plane Images
Amadeus Aviation

The descriptions and characteristics of the helicopters in this book are based on a combination of personal experience and open source material and the author and publisher disclaim any liability to any party for loss, damage or disruption caused by errors or omissions whether made by accident or negligence.

Glossary

Aerobatics Exciting manoeuvres involving going upside down or looping the loop and steep turns.

Altitude Height above sea level as opposed to 'height' which is height above the ground.

Autorotation A term which describes the undesirable flight condition encountered when the engines stop! Once established in autorotation, however, it is relatively easy to control the helicopter and land it safely.

Avionics A generic term to describe the electrical control systems and instruments in an aircraft.

BERP British Experimental Rotor Programme – which designed an excellent blade enabling very high forward speeds as well as much improved hover performance.

Coaxial A term which describes rotor blades mounted one above the other – see the Helix.

Composite A term which in a general sense describes aircraft structures not made of metal, for example carbon fibre or Kevlar.

Compound A description of a helicopter which uses propellers and rotor blades in flight.

Counter rotating or coaxial blades An arrangement whereby one set of rotors sits above the other to reduce overall footprint of the aircraft and to eliminate torque effect.

Downwash The wind generated by a helicopter when hovering. If you stand under one you will know all about it!

Dual A cockpit arrangement whereby the pilots sit side by side.

Elastomeric bearings	Bearings generally used in the rotor head, that use an elastic material to allow movement instead of metal bearings. This reduces the number of parts required and reduces maintenance.
Endurance	The amount of time a helicopter can remain airborne.
FADEC	Fully Automated Digital Engine Control. A system where no matter how the pilot pushes and pulls on the engine control levers, a computer will decide how much fuel to allow into the engine. This greatly reduces the chances of damaging engines during starting. It can be over-ridden in emergency situations.
Fenestron	A tail rotor arrangement whereby the tail rotor is contained inside the tail fin as opposed to being mounted on the side. See Gazelle and Dauphin.
Fixed wing	An aircraft where the wings do not move – an aeroplane to you and me.
Frigate	Smaller class of naval battleship.
Fuselage	The main body of the aircraft onto which engines, gearboxes, seats, and so on, are fixed.
Gatling gun	A design of cannon that overcomes barrel overheating problems by using three or more barrels which rotate, firing one after the other.
Glass cockpit	A term used to describe a cockpit where square glass screens are used for the instrument displays rather than separate round dials.
Heavy	A heavy helicopter is any machine above approximately 20 tonnes.
Hellfire missile	A missile manufactured by Lockheed Martin principally designed as an anti-tank weapon with a range of up to 8 km.
Helmet mounted display	Either a visor or monocle device which can display flight instrument or night vision imagery directly to the pilot without the need to look down at screens or dials.
Hook	This generally refers to the cargo hook found on the bottom of utility helicopters.
Intermeshing blades	Blades which are positioned such that when they turn they intermesh – see K-Max helicopter.

Knot – nautical mile per hour	The speed an aircraft flies measured with respect to a nautical mile which allows for the curvature of the earth whereas a statute mile is slightly shorter because it is a true straight line.
Laser-guided	A means of guiding a missile by using a laser which the pilot, or a soldier on the ground, points at the target – the missile follows the laser. Often referred to as 'laser designation'.
Light	A light helicopter is any machine up to approximately 5 tonnes.
Max all up mass – MAUM	The maximum weight that the helicopter can take off at including all fuel, equipment and people.
MEDEVAC	Medical evacuation – a term used to describe air ambulance helicopters.
Medium	A medium helicopter is any machine up to approximately 20 tonnes.
Missile	A weapon that can be guided in-flight onto a target where it detonates.
NOTAR	An abbreviation meaning 'no tail rotor', a common example being the MD900 series which uses a blast of air instead of a tail rotor to keep the aircraft from spinning.
Offset tail rotor blades	Tail rotors generally either have four or two equally spaced blades, however some have four blades which are spaced unevenly to accommodate control rods – they are known as offset blades. It is rumoured this arrangement reduces noise too – see Apache.
Para-public	A term which describes activities such as police, fire and search and rescue work.
Payload	The amount of cargo a helicopter can carry.
Puller/pusher	A description of a propeller which either pushes the aircraft along or pulls it along.
Rocket	A weapon which has no guidance once it has been fired: it detonates where it lands.
Rotary wing	An aircraft where the wings go round – a helicopter to you and me.
Rotor head	The assembly on the top of a helicopter where the rotor blades attach.
Servo	An electric or hydraulically-powered device which moves flight controls according to pilot control inputs.

Single engine/twin engine	Different machines have different numbers of engines; two engines are considered safer so that in the event of one failing the remaining engine is capable of either maintaining level flight or at least cushioning the impact!
Solo	Either an aircraft with only one seat or a term to describe an aircraft being flown with only one pilot.
Survivability	A measure of how difficult a helicopter is to shoot down.
Tailwind	Wind coming from the rear of the aircraft, particularly relevant to machines with a tail rotor which suffer from large power demands when they experience tailwinds on landing. Other designs such as coaxial, tandem or intermeshing blades are largely immune to tailwinds.
Tandem	A cockpit arrangement whereby the pilots sit one in front of the other. Similarly, a tandem rotor layout is where the blades are positioned one set in front of the other (see CH47 Chinook).
Tilt rotor	A machine which has rotors which can operate both horizontally like a normal helicopter and also tilt forwards to become propellers like an aeroplane.
Torque effect	When the main rotor on an aircraft turns, it grips the air which causes the aircraft to climb and also causes the aircraft itself to want to spin in the opposite direction to the blades; this is the 'torque effect' which is cancelled either by a tail rotor or some other blade arrangement – see counter-rotating blades or intermeshing blades.
Turboshaft	A design of gas turbine engine commonly used in helicopters which is designed to produce rotation power rather than thrust like a jet engine.
Weapons pylons	The mounts on the small wings of an attack helicopter to which weapons and fuel pods are fitted.

A129 Mangusta

Leonardo

Assembled and/or manufactured in: Italy

A smaller attack helicopter of which only 110 have been made, operated by the Italian and Turkish armed forces. Whilst not immediately obvious to even the informed observer, it shares a lot of components with the A109. The tail section is where most parts are shared. Despite its lack of overall stature (4,600 kg max all up mass) it does boast an impressive variety of weapon and sensor capabilities – it is capable of firing 8 km range Hellfire missiles, for example. Great thought has been applied to minimising pilot workload with many systems (weapons and flight) controlled directly by onboard computers. Variants suitable for maritime and scouting roles have been proposed but demand has yet to warrant these being built.

Powered by two Rolls-Royce Gem turboshaft engines, 890 horse power each.

A129 Mangusta:
downed aircrew extraction

AW119 Koala

Leonardo

Assembled and/or manufactured in: Italy

This simple modern helicopter defies the prevailing wisdom that two engines are better than one. The larger single-engine design enables great economies of scale as only one set of governors are required, one fuel system, one engine control system, and so on. The result is a relatively inexpensive machine which has remarkable cabin capacity for its class. Whilst it has similar lift capabilities to the Squirrel, it can carry three more passengers – and in comfort. It has proved very popular as a police and ambulance helicopter in less densely populated areas where single-engine operations are not a concern. With additional fuel tanks it is capable of remaining airborne for up to 6 hours.

Powered by one Pratt & Whitney PT6B-37A turbine engine, 1,000 horse power.

AW119 Koala clearly showing its
A109 origins in profile

AW101 (EH101)

Leonardo
Assembled and/or manufactured in: UK and Italy

Described as a medium lift helicopter this machine is impressively fast and arguably has some heavy lift characteristics such as the capacity to carry 45 troops. It is particularly fast across the battlefield, cruising at 150 knots and can remain airborne for 5 hours. Part of its performance is due to the BERP rotor blades which are identifiable by the paddle shapes on the ends of the rotors. It has succeeded primarily as a military aircraft selling to some 11 countries, though search and rescue variants have also been made.

Powered by three Rolls-Royce Turbomeca RTM322 engines, up to 2,200 horse power each.

AW101 (EH101) Merlin

Eurocopter Tiger

Sitting somewhere in between the Apache AH64D and Mangusta, the Tiger is an exceptionally modern composite constructed helicopter. It is highly agile and whilst not as narrow as a Cobra it has an impressively slim fuselage making it difficult to see head-on. Despite being a technically advanced machine its development has been beset with commercial and political difficulties, being born out of a French/German collaboration in the midst of uncertain state finances. It has also experienced some difficulties in its export sales, however, it has since proven itself in combat with more than four different countries. The helmet-mounted display integrates with all aircraft systems and enables high fidelity binocular night vision as opposed to the Apache monocular system. Whilst it lacks the sheer bulk and lifting ability of an Apache or Havoc, it makes up for it with the latest on-board technology.

Powered by two Turbomeca Rolls-Royce MTR390 turboshaft engines, 1,300 horse power each.

EC665 Tiger

Cobra AH-1/ AH-1W/AH-1Z

Bell Helicopters

Assembled and/or manufactured in: USA

It is amazing quite how narrow this helicopter is. Even the lightly built pilot wears the Cobra snuggly about the shoulders. This simple but vital characteristic makes it extremely difficult to see the Cobra head-on and is a massive aid to survivability. It has enjoyed extensive upgrades from its single engine twin-bladed origins (AH-1) to a highly agile four-bladed twin engine (AH-1Z Viper or 'Zulu' Cobra). It can carry similar weapons to the Apache, such as Hellfire missiles and 70 mm rockets combined with a 20 mm Gatling cannon. As can be seen from this picture, its design origins come from the venerable Huey. It started life in 1965 as a Huey with the cockpit and cabin removed in favour of a tandem cockpit and weapons pylons.

Powered by two General Electric T700 CT7 turbine engines, 1,600 horse power each.

**AH-1W Super Cobra –
US Marine Corps**

AW169

Leonardo

Assembled and/or manufactured in: Italy and USA

This is the most modern helicopter to feature in this book having only received its European Aviation Safety Agency clearance to fly in July 2015. At 4.5 tonnes it fills an interesting gap in the market between its smaller 3-tonne cousin the AW109 and the larger 6.5-tonne AW139. As such it offers a meaningful 10-person capacity for transport operations or a very spacious cabin for six VIPs, the latter no doubt benefitting from not spilling their drinks thanks to the highly advanced blade vibration damping systems. The first sale was to a VIP customer in September 2015 with Lease Corporation International ordering 12 more in October 2015 and the first air ambulance version has been bought by Kent Surrey and Sussex Air Ambulance. Sleek, powerful and flexible, it looks set to become a sales success.

Powered by two Pratt & Whitney PW210A FADEC turboshaft engines.

AW169

CH-47
Chinook

Boeing
Assembled and/or
manufactured in: USA

A fantastic machine to which countless soldiers owe their lives. Its ability to fly fast (170 knots) and quickly thump onto the ground with no fuss come day, night, snow, dust, wind or rain and then gather up tens of heavily armed soldiers and/or casualties makes it the ultimate military helicopter. Its tandem rotor layout is hugely efficient and makes it largely immune to the effects of adverse wind when landing. It has developed over the years in power and speed to such an extent that it can lift some 10 tonnes and later versions have almost 10,000 horse power available. In short, this machine is a beast that will take any amount of abuse and keep on flying.

Powered by two Honeywell T55-715 engines (later models only).

CH-47 conducting pinnacle
landing training

Rooivalk CSH2

This is one helicopter that you are unlikely to see because only 12 have ever been built and one of those has been crashed beyond repair. Nevertheless, it is an interesting machine which has a lot of Super Puma DNA in its design and components taken from the Atlas Oryx; itself a Puma derived helicopter. It has only seen limited operational flying in the Democratic Republic of Congo where it fired its 20 mm cannon. It now has a guided missile system and has had a software upgrade. It is no longer in production having failed to win overseas orders.

Powered by two Turbomeca Makila 1K2 turboshaft engines, 1,900 horse power each.

Rooivalk CSH2

KMAX series

Kaman aircraft
Assembled and/or
manufactured in: USA

Not the prettiest flying machine, but certainly one that outperforms almost all helicopters in terms of efficiency and lift. It is capable of lifting almost 120 per cent of its body weight which even the load-lugging Chinook cannot compete with. The unusual intermeshing rotor arrangement is the source of the efficiency. All of the power goes into vertical lift with none wasted in tail rotor systems. Furthermore, hydraulics and heavy pitch change mechanisms are not required because small manually controlled flaps (visible in the outer part of the main blades) on the blades alter the angle rather than powered servos. For its intended low-speed high-lift operations, this is the perfect control arrangement. It is also one of a very few machines that have been successfully flown unmanned – in this instance performing aerial resupply work in Afghanistan.

Powered by one Honeywell T53-17 turboshaft engine, 1,800 horse power.

K-1200 KMAX

SH-2 Seasprite

Kaman aircraft

Assembled and/or manufactured in: USA

The Seasprite was designed in the 1950s as a US Navy utility helicopter though it did not really come to life until 1968 when it was rebuilt with two engines along with the addition of anti-submarine and anti-surface capabilities. The reason for its longevity as a US Navy aircraft was that it was small enough to fit onto the frigates in service at the time, whereas the bigger, more capable Seahawk UH60 would not fit. Once the US Navy fleet was upgraded to larger frigates in 1993, the rationale for keeping the Seasprite in service faded and it was replaced by the Seahawk UH60. In 1997, the SH-2G Super Seasprite was selected by the Australian Navy as its intermediate helicopter, however, after 11 years of failing to meet the Australian Navy requirements the project was scrapped in 2008 after large cost increases and delays.

Powered by two T700 GE 401/401C turboshaft engines, up to 1,285 horse power each.

SH-2F Seasprite preparing to land on USS Nicholson

KA50/52
Hokum

Kamov
Assembled and/or
manufactured in: Russia

This helicopter certainly looks menacing and as its nicknames of 'Alligator', 'Werewolf' and 'Black Shark' suggest, it is not a MEDEVAC machine! The counter rotating blades make it highly manoeuvrable and remove the need for a delicate and power hungry tail rotor. The theory behind the single cockpit is that the attack phases of flight – low-level navigation, target acquisition and attack – happen one after the other and therefore only one pilot is needed. In my experience, those tasks tend to overlap a great deal and I would not envy the task facing a KA50 pilot during full combat. It is telling that the KA52 now has two seats which, unusually for an attack helicopter, are side by side. What is truly unique about the Hokum is the ejection seat. Before the pilots eject, the blades are blown off by explosives and the pilots are then ejected vertically.

Powered by two Klimov VK-2500 turbine engines, 1,750 horse power each.

Two KA50s flying over Moscow

KA-27
Helix

Kamov

Assembled and/or
manufactured in: Russia

Despite being a popular choice amongst Russian orientated countries as a military helicopter, you are quite likely to see this machine working in central Europe as a civilian variant. I have seen one lifting ski-lift equipment in Switzerland and one putting out fires in Cyprus. It is popular as a navy variant due to its compact dimensions compared to tail rotor aircraft. Like all coaxial helicopters, it is immune from the performance loss that tail rotor machines suffer with tailwinds. The coaxial blade arrangement enables precise handling in the hover which is a characteristic much valued by navy pilots landing on small ships at night. The cabin layout lends itself to accommodating additional crew to operate the wide array of radar systems which have been fitted to the naval variants around the world.

Powered by two Isotov TV3-117V turboshaft engines, up to 2,230 horse power each.

KA-27 Helix from the destroyer
Admiral Vinogradov

BK-117

Messerschmitt-Bölkow-Blohm (MBB) and Kawasaki

Assembled and/or manufactured in: Germany and Japan

This is the predecessor of the H145 which also features in this book. It was born in the late 1970s out of an unusual collaboration between MBB of Germany and Kawasaki of Japan. The helicopter was made in both countries though development was split across the two, with Japan designing the majority of the fuselage structure and controls and Germany the rotating parts. Of the 443 BK-117s made, some 329 were made in Germany and 111 in Japan. Initial development and certification took longer than expected but once cleared in the USA, this machine's potential as a utility/law enforcement/ambulance helicopter was never in doubt.

Powered by two Textron Lycoming LTS 101-750B-1 turboshaft engines, 593 horse power each.

**BK-117 of the North-Rhine
Westphalia Police in Germany**

Mi-28 Havoc

Mil Helicopters

Assembled and/or manufactured in: Russia

This is the Eastern bloc response to the Apache; whilst the looks are different the attributes and layout are very similar, right down to the offset blades on the tail rotor. The most significant difference is the inclusion of a three-man passenger pod for the purpose of rescuing downed air crew. This appears to be a carry-over from the 'Hind' Mi-24 helicopter which has a compartment for armed assault troops. The on-board sensors and weapons array mimic the Apache closely though it could be argued the Havoc is a more robust machine, weighing approximately two tonnes more than the Apache.

Weapons include: rockets (laser-guided and free flight), missiles (four variants), 30 mm cannon (550 rounds per minute).

Powered by two Klimov TV3-117 turboshaft engines, up to 2,194 horse power each.

Mi-28N

Mi-26

Mil Helicopters
Assembled and/or
manufactured in: Russia

This helicopter has to be included quite simply because it is the biggest conventional helicopter ever made. The figures are bewildering – it weighs 56 tonnes when fully loaded and can carry 90 soldiers or 20 tonnes of cargo and achieve 159 knots forward speed. Despite or because of its immensity, it is in service with a surprising number of countries around the world, from central Europe to South America to Africa. It can produce a little under 23,000 horse power from its two engines and employs a novel design of torque-splitting gearbox to cope with this huge power output. Its eight blades are so big it is possible to walk along the main rotors to conduct inspections. Unlike some of its 'attack' Russian brothers and despite its bulk, it is an elegant and almost graceful aircraft.

Powered by two Lotarev D-136 turboshaft engines, 11,400 horse power each.

Mi-26

X3 (EC155)

Eurocopter/Airbus
Assembled and/or
manufactured in: France

Whilst you are unlikely to see this machine as it only exists in experimental form, it deserves mention because it develops an old concept of increasing the maximum speed by the use of 'puller' rotors – otherwise known as a compound helicopter. The puller or 'tractor' blades are driven directly from the main gearbox. It has successfully flown at some 250 knots (about 100 knots quicker than a fast conventional helicopter). This advantage will allow it to compete with private jets for shorter journeys without the need to take off or land at an airport. Production plans have not been confirmed though Airbus indicate that 2020 could see the start of manufacture. Their main market is the oil and gas offshore sector where shorter duration transits will boost productivity.

Powered by two Rolls-Royce RTM322 turbine engines, up to 2,200 horse power each.

Eurocopter X3 at Marignane,
France

AW609 TiltRotor

Leonardo
Assembled and/or
manufactured in: USA

Another interesting take on the tilt rotor concept. This is, in basic terms, a smaller version of the V22 Osprey and benefits from all of the learning gained during the V22 development. Like any tilt rotor it offers a large speed advantage (275 knots) over conventional helicopters (150 knots) whilst not requiring a landing strip. However, being that much smaller, the AW609 is less intrusive in terms of noise and downwash which makes it a more practical proposal for working from city heliports and oil rig landing pads. Unlike other tilt rotors, the 609 is capable of autorotating safely to ground with no engine power. Leonardo envisage oil and gas as the primary market with Bristow Helicopters taking a significant interest, however at the time of writing, the programme has been delayed by a fatal crash which killed two test pilots.

Powered by two Pratt & Whitney PT6C-67A turboshaft engines, up to 1,900 horse power each.

AW609

Sikorsky
S-300

Hughes/Schweizer
Assembled and/or
manufactured in: USA

A design which first flew in the 1950s and became a commercial success in the 1960s in the roles of flying training, police and agriculture. These days, it is more limited to flying training as the role in agriculture is limited to mustering and the police now require greater payloads and endurance. The latest model, the 300CBi features fuel injection to remove the risk of carburettor icing. It is favoured as a training aircraft due to the stability imparted by its three-bladed main rotor and its forgiving handling during take off and landing. Its generous cockpit space makes for a more comfortable machine with space for three large adults.

Powered by one Lycoming HIO-360-D1A piston engine, 190 horse power.

Schweizer 300C

Westland WS-61 Sea King series

Westland Helicopters
Assembled and/or manufactured in: UK under licence from Sikorsky

I cannot think of another helicopter that will have saved so many lives around the world. The Sea King does not go fast, it does not do backflips and it does not fire much by way of weapons, but since 1969 it has flown in atrocious weather for huge distances pulling terrified people out of desperate situations. Its most famous livery in the UK is in RAF yellow, as seen by countless stranded walkers, climbers and sailors. It is unusual in many ways, but two attributes jump out, namely its ability to swim on water – note the boat-shaped hull under the cockpit, and the facility for the rear crew man to conduct precision close quarter hovering via additional controls in the rear cabin. The latter makes it perfect for hovering over stricken boats whilst winching is under way.

Powered by two Rolls-Royce Gnome H1400-2-turboshaft engines, up to 1,660 horse power each.

Sea King HAR3A

MBB BO105

An unassuming-looking machine which has the most extraordinary handling capabilities. This machine wins aerobatics competitions open to fixed-wing entries. Its agility comes from a remarkable forged titanium rotor head which means it can fly upside down for short periods without any of the blade deflection concerns that an articulated rotor head would bring. It has a powerful hydraulic system which twists the titanium in order to manoeuvre the blades in pitch. It has been a highly popular air ambulance and civil police aircraft as well as serving around the world in army, navy and air force roles. Now approaching 45 years old, it is largely being withdrawn from service with no competitor coming close to its manoeuvrability.

Powered by two Allison 250-C20B turboshaft engines, rated at 420 horse power each.

Indonesian BO105

SA330 Puma

Aerospatiale/Airbus
Assembled and/or
manufactured in: France

A machine that has stood the test of time, originating in 1963, new variants are still being made and many older machines are still flying. It has served in the Royal Air Force for some 44 years and has recently had a life extension with the addition of a glass cockpit, improved engines and transmission upgrades. Its most simple attributes are its best: large cabin doors and a large flat load area. It was designed from the outset as a military machine and has survivability inbuilt. During the 1970s, it was the best-selling transport helicopter, equally popular on oil rig duties as military. Care is required when parking as it is possible to come back to your Puma to find it lying on its side if there are strong winds and you failed to tie it down.

Powered by two Turbomecca Turmo turbine engines, 1,500 horse power each.

HC1 33 Squadron RAF.
Bardufoss, Norway

UH1 Iroquois series

Bell Helicopters
Assembled and/or
manufactured in: USA

This is the machine that proved the utility of the helicopter as a war machine. Until then, helicopters had been overly complex, unreliable and did not offer a useful payload and range combination. The UH1 or 'Huey' changed all of that with a robust, simple and enormously reliable machine that won the hearts of US troops in Vietnam. It was significantly developed from the UH1-A which entered service in 1962, to the UH-1E which only went fully out of service with US forces in 2015. Payload and seating greatly increased over the years. The twin-bladed arrangement makes for a very distinctive thudding sound in flight which was either hugely reassuring or alarming depending on whether you were friend or foe.

Powered by one Lycoming T53-L-1 (770 horse power) through to a T53-L-13 (1,400 horse power).

UH-1D Helicopters lift 2nd Battalion 14th Infantry Regiment during a search and destroy mission in Vietnam in 1966

AW139

Leonardo
Assembled and/or manufactured in: Italy and USA

Another cleverly positioned helicopter in terms of its weight and capacity. It was originally designated as the AB139 – the B reflecting the joint design venture with Bell Helicopters but, after a buy-out, it is now the AW139. In its short life (first certified in 2003) it has proved very popular with the oil and gas industry due to its range (620 miles), speed (160 knots) and capacity (15 seated passengers). I flew an early production version in 2003 and was very impressed by the level automation and the available power even with full fuel and several passengers. It has since proved itself as an excellent search and rescue machine due to its ability to have a huge variety of equipment fitted, such as winches, thermal cameras, radar, anti-ice protection and lights.

Powered by two Pratt & Whitney PT6C-67C turboshaft engines, 1,531 horse power each.

AW139

EC(H)145

Eurocopter/Airbus
Assembled and/or
manufactured in: Germany

This might not sound like the most complimentary description, but the EC145, now the H145, is truly the Transit van of the skies. It is an enormously adaptable machine that can take a large variety of external equipment whilst also having a supremely flexible load space. Clever routing of the control cables means the side doors open wider than would otherwise be possible and the rear clam shell doors make access even easier. It affords an excellent view to the pilot and is simple to jump in and start as required by any ambulance operator. Such is its flexibility, the US Army have selected it as its prime utility machine (named UH-72A Lakota) against strong USA-based competition.

Powered by two Turbomeca Arriel 2E engines.

EC145

Dauphin

Eurocopter/Airbus
Assembled and/or
manufactured in: France

Another machine which combines elegance with practical utility design, much like the A109 but slightly bigger. The large fenestron tail gives excellent stability in forward flight but can increase the pilot workload when hovering 'cross wind'. The Dauphin broke away from its corporate or VIP image when in 1979, the US Coastguard selected it and bought the HH-65 Dolphin for short-range recovery. It also fulfils the unusual role of *non signature aviation support* to the UK SAS, having taken over from the venerable Argentinian A109As. It also exists as a military variant: the AS565 Panther.

Powered by two Arriel 2C turbine engines.

AS365N3

MD900
series

McDonnell Douglas
Assembled and/or
manufactured in: USA

This is the machine that truly brought NOTAR (no tail rotor) into the mainstream of aviation; it was designed from the outset not to have a conventional tail rotor. Whilst tail authority is not quite what it would be with a large four-bladed rotor, it makes much less noise and is considerably safer for passengers entering and exiting the aircraft. The NOTAR also makes it perfect for landing in tight spaces in built-up areas. Should the pilot misjudge the landing point, the worst that can happen is a dent in the tail cone as opposed to destroying the tail rotor and firing debris over any onlookers. It uses a blast of air from the end of the tail to control which way the nose points as well as having a cleverly shaped tail boom which also generates sideways thrust.

Powered by two Pratt & Whitney Canada PW206A turbine engines, 550 horse power each.

MD900 Explorer

Gazelle SA 340-342

Aerospatiale/Airbus
Assembled and/or manufactured in: France

Also built under license by AugustaWestland/ Leonardo at Yeovil UK

A single-engine light reconnaissance helicopter which is highly agile and has good 'hot and high' performance. A simple and exciting machine to fly, it has been employed extensively by the UK and French military in training and active service roles. In its role as a scouting helicopter, it would fly ahead of Lynx Mk 7 helicopters on anti-tank missions and was the primary source of overhead reconnaissance for troops in Northern Ireland. Because of its sleek appearance, speed, agility and simple design, it is a popular civilian machine despite being relatively thirsty for its weight class.

Weapons have included: 20 mm cannon, Mistral air-to-air missile, HOT air-to-surface missile.

Sights and sensors include: Gazelle Observation Aid (GOA), boom- and roof-mounted thermal sights.

Powered by an Astazou turbine engine with exceptional reliability, 700 horse power.

Regiment Army Air Corp Gazelle Helicopter MOD

A109 series

Leonardo
Assembled and/or
manufactured in: Italy

Great designs never look old and the A109 is a brilliant example of this. The design you see here dates from 1971 yet still looks as elegant as it did then. The A109 is best known as a corporate or VIP helicopter, a role it is well suited to by dint of its looks, flat-out speed (160 knots) and smooth ride. Despite this reputation, it is also in demand as a military and 'para-public' helicopter. It is capable of having a wide array of role equipment fitted and is in service with numerous armed forces as well as the US Coastguard. One unusual role is that of UK counterterrorist operations in support of the Special Air Service. This role was carried out for many years by a fleet of four A109s – two of which were 'requisitioned' from the Argentine Air Force in 1982.

Powered by two Pratt & Whitney PW207 turbine engines, 560 horse power each.

A109 Grande

EC135 / H135

Eurocopter/Airbus Helicopters

Assembled and/or manufactured in: Germany

A well-considered design which accurately met the rising demand for air ambulance and police support tasks in the late 1990s across Europe and further afield. The cabin layout, with an entirely flat floor, wide sliding doors and rear access clam shell doors makes it perfect for single stretcher casualties. It has quickly become the default setting for air ambulance operators. The skidded undercarriage lends itself well to attaching observation devices, cameras, searchlights and speakers, all of which enhance its utility in para-public roles. Single-pilot day, night and instrument certification further adds to its capability.

Powered by two Turbomeca Arrius 2B or Pratt & Whitney PW208B engines.

EC135 T2 at Wattisham Airfield

AS355 series 'Squirrel'

Airbus/Eurocopter

Assembled and/or
manufactured in: France

Known as the *A Star* in the USA, where it has sold in huge numbers, this machine made great advances in reducing parts count and thereby reducing maintenance costs when it came out in 1977. Its claim to fame comes from the B3 variant which proved superb as a high altitude machine; in 2005, a 'B3' landed on the summit of Mount Everest. Brave and skilled pilots supported by this excellent mountain helicopter have been able to rescue many climbers who would have perished had it not been for this remarkable machine. A variant of the B2 took over from its predecessor, the Gazelle, as the UK Armed Forces training helicopter – a role in which it has proved highly dependable. There are approximately 3,500 'Squirrels' in service around the world.

Powered by one Arriel 1-D-1 turbine engine, approximately 800 horse power.

**AS350B2 Ecureuil,
Denham Airfield**

V-22 Osprey

Bell/Boeing
Assembled and/or
manufactured in: USA

An extraordinary machine that, whilst it does not quite conform to the definition of a helicopter, is certainly worthy of mention in this book. Despite costing double the equivalent sized helicopter and not being able to lift as much, it more than makes up for this by flying at 275 knots, some 100 knots faster than the fastest helicopters. It has a ferocious downdraft and a very distinctive noise, both of which limit its utility in close combat situations but as a means of delivering troops and equipment to remote, unprepared sites it is unbeatable by conventional fixed or rotary wing machines.

Powered by two Rolls-Royce AE 1107C engines, 6,000 horse power each.

V-22 Osprey, Wilmington, NC

Jet Ranger 206/306B

Bell Helicopters
Assembled and/or manufactured in: USA

A design which has stood the test of time and derives much of its DNA from the legendary Huey of the same brand. The simple main and tail rotor design gives long life and minimal maintenance with only a slight penalty in terms of agility and flat-out speed. The passenger space is impressive for such a small helicopter and it has proved itself hugely successful as a commercial helicopter for all manner of tasks, from law enforcement to pipeline inspection to passenger flying. There is also a military variant called the Kiowa which is used for reconnaissance. The Alison C250 engine has proved enormously reliable as demonstrated by this helicopter being the first to fly around the world in 1982.

Powered by a single Alison C250 series turbine engine.

G-SUEY

B206

Bell 212 Twin Huey

Bell/Boeing
Assembled and/or
manufactured in: USA

A direct descendant of the legendary Huey with all the rugged attributes of that machine but with the benefit of an additional engine and superior avionics. It is capable of carrying 15 seated passengers and as a result was ideal for commercial roles such as oil and gas exploration. It proved to be a highly successful medium utility machine, popular for a wide variety of rescue and emergency operations such as firefighting, search and rescue, ambulance and law enforcement. It is now over 40 years old and is largely being removed from service but is still operated by the UK Army Air Corps in jungle warfare training support roles where its stable hovering and high power margins have made it an ideal machine for approaching tight jungle clearings much as its predecessor did in Vietnam.

Powered by two Pratt & Whitney PT6T-3 turbine engines, 900 horse power each.

Bell 212, UK Army Air Corps, Brunei

Apache AH-64D

Boeing Aircraft Corporation
Assembled and/or manufactured in: USA

Also built under licence by AugustaWestland at Yeovil UK

Boeing's Apache was born out of American experience in Vietnam which demonstrated the need for a heavily armed and protected attack helicopter. The answer came in the form of the Apache and the 'D' model combines a variety of aggressive weapons, excellent crew protection, a large array of high technology sensors and impressive endurance.

Weapons include: Hellfire missiles (8 km), CRV7 rockets (8 km) and 30 mm cannon (3 km).

Sights and sensors include: millimetric radar, enemy radar detection, enemy missile launch detection, thermal sights, optical sights, laser range finding and designation.

Power for the UK model is provided by two Rolls-Royce RTM322 turboshaft engines, 2,200 horse power each.

**Army Air Corps Apache Helicopter Pilot
Prepares for Take Off**

S-64 series

Sikorsky–Erikson
Assembled and/or
manufactured in: USA

Created by Sikorsky but developed by Erikson. This highly specialised aerial crane is instantly recognisable and fascinates me. One distinctive feature is that the rear-facing crewman has a duplicate set of controls for flying the hook onto loads. These machines perform vital lifesaving firefighting duties and, as a result, individual aircraft such as 'Elvis', an orange firefighting variant based in Australia, have become renowned. Its 10,000-litre fire retardant tank gives it real firefighting capability as its payload can be dropped with more accuracy than is possible with a fixed wing firefighter. The snorkel arrangement enables rapid refills from even quite small water sources such as ponds and swimming pools where conventional buckets would not function.

Powered by two Pratt & Whitney T73-P-700 engines, 4,800 horse power each.

Erikson Sky Crane S-64

Hughes/ MD500 series

McDonnell Douglas
Assembled and/or
manufactured in: USA

Also built under licence by
Kawasaki Heavy Industries
Japan

A single-engine light reconnaissance helicopter owing its origins to the Vietnam war. One of the most fun and agile machines it is possible to fly. The high number of main rotor blades and compact dimensions make it unusually responsive. The 'Angry Egg' has developed considerably from its incarnation as the 'OH-6' with the unique feature for such a small machine of having a six-bladed variant and it has been adapted to unmanned flight. Due to its continued development and attractive pricing it is popular with smaller armies as well as being a top-selling private transport machine. 'Magnum PI' famously brought this machine to the wider public's attention in the 1980s.

Powered by the Allison 250-C series, 280 horse power, with exceptional reliability.

MD500E

Mi-24, 25 and 35 series

Mil

Assembled and/or manufactured in: Former USSR

A brute of a machine which uniquely combines a troop carry capability into a dedicated attack helicopter. Many utility machines have had weapons added but this is a true attack machine that can also carry eight assault troops. Its cramped cockpits with unusual ergonomics are a step back for most western pilots but its weapons array and survivability are world class. Known as the 'Hind', its profile is distinctive and menacing. It has been a very successful export model for Mil, selling to some 55 countries and is even piloted by a private security company in West Africa.

Powered by two Izotov TV3-177A turboshaft engines, 2,200 horse power each.

Mi-24

Mi8/17

Mi8/17 Helicopters
Assembled and/or
manufactured in: Former
USSR

Spurred on by the huge success of the American Bell UH-1, the Soviet military pressed for their own version and the Mi8 was the result. It started out as a single-engine machine but for reasons of reliability it soon became apparent that two would be required. It has capacity for 24 troops and can be armed with a variety of weapons and ancillary equipment. The cockpit is a thing to behold for a western pilot: there is acres of space and an array of dials in what seem unlikely places. The 'greenhouse' glazing affords a good view but lends it an old-fashioned look. The design has proved hugely successful and with over 17,000 having been built, it is the third most common military aircraft in the world and it is still in production despite starting life in 1961. It also flies around the world as a civil variant.

Powered by two Isotov TV2 engines, 1,500 horse power each.

Mi8

Robinson R22

Robinson Helicopters
Assembled and/or
manufactured in: USA

A brilliant design which put helicopter flying within the financial reach of a new market previously excluded by the cost of buying and running a helicopter. The R22 addressed both of these issues whilst providing a machine that is exceptionally agile, manoeuvrable and fun to fly. It is certainly a little twitchy when first flown but nothing that cannot be mastered by 'relaxing' on the controls more. The design is hugely efficient with clever weight-saving measures such as a single set of control linkages married to a unique dual control yoke, the result being weight reduction, maintenance reduction and fewer parts required. It is popular as a trainer and for mustering livestock on large properties.

Powered by a single Lycoming O-320-B2C piston engine, 124 horse power.

R22

CH53/CH53E/MH53 – Jolly Green Giant

Sikorsky
Assembled and/or manufactured in: USA

A more impressive and imposing machine you will struggle to find. Powered by a total of three engines and possessing seven main rotor blades this machine can lift 55 troops and fly nearly 1,200 statute miles. Its automatic blade folding is a device of wonder and enables it to fold its wings and descend into the lower deck of an aircraft carrier. The hydraulics and ingenuity to make all this work defy belief. It started out as a twin-engine machine in 1964 and sprouted a third engine in 1974 in response to US military demands for more lifting capacity. Its tilted tail fin enables the tail rotor to contribute to keeping the machine level in the hover whilst also maintaining a level altitude in forward flight. Another unusual feature is the in-flight refuel probe. Cool nerves are required for refuelling helicopters in-flight; a quick Internet search will show you videos of what can go wrong.

Powered by three General Electric T64-GE-416-416A turboshaft engines, approximately 4,300 horse power each.

CH53E on board USS Bataan

Sikorsky UH60 series

Sikorsky

Assembled and/or manufactured in: USA

Another Vietnam product which addressed the observation that loss of circulating fluids (fuel, coolant, lubrication, hydraulics, blood) causes helicopters to crash. This machine was a huge step forward in addressing that problem. Along with the Apache, it makes best use of the rugged tricycle undercarriage which offers enhanced stability in harsh landings often encountered in dust whilst using night vision devices. This aircraft has a superb reputation for toughness and reliability. When teamed up with British AH64Ds in Afghanistan, its crews saved numerous coalition lives in the most unlikely and demanding scenarios. In its latest incarnation, it was this machine that delivered Seal Team 6 operatives to Abbotabad to apprehend Osama bin Laden in 2011.

Powered by two T700-GE701C engines, 1,800 horse power each.

MH60 at Ghila Bend Air Force ranges, Arizona, USA

Sikorsky S76 series

Sikorsky

Assembled and/or manufactured in: USA

The S76 was born, to an extent, from the UH60 Blackhawk series but was always designed and intended as a civil aircraft primarily aimed at the offshore oil and gas industries. This particular one serves an interesting role as one of the UK Royal flight, seen here transporting Prince Charles whilst presenting Afghanistan medals to my former Army Air Corps unit. Owing to its sleek profile, it set range and speed class records when it emerged in 1982. Its single piece aluminium rotor head with elastomeric bearings vastly reduced the parts count and increased servicing intervals. Due to its spacious cabin and low levels of vibration it is particularly popular in the corporate and VIP market.

Latest variant S-76C+ powered by two Turbomeca Arriel 2S2 engines, 922 horse power each.

S76C-2 Wattisham Airfield, 2011

Lynx Mk 7

Westland
Assembled and/or
manufactured in: UK

Second only to the BO105 in terms of agility, the semi-rigid forged titanium rotor head gives this machine superbly responsive handling. Rotor speed control can catch pilots out at low power settings. Very few machines can match its ability to back flip from the hover or loop or barrel roll. On top of that, it still holds the world helicopter speed record of 249 mph. Most of my 1,000 hours on this machine were spent in Northern Ireland where it proved perfect for squeezing between hedgerows or under wires on foggy nights in South Armagh.

Powered by two Rolls-Royce GEM 41-1 engines, 1,120 horse power each.

Lynx Mk 7

SE3130
Alouette II

Sud Aviation, later Aerospatiale

Assembled and/or manufactured in: France

A record-breaking high altitude helicopter, as indicated by this photograph taken in the Swiss Alps. In the mid to late 1950s the Alouette II made history by achieving an altitude record of 10,984 metres (36,027 ft) and the first successful rescue above 4,000 metres. It has proved an extremely popular scout helicopter for over 47 armed forces around the world with a notable presence in Africa. Its final version was the Indian-manufactured version, the SA315B Lama which regularly conducted missions in the Indian Himalayas. The design gave rise to the equally successful Gazelle which succeeded it.

Powered by one Turbomeca Artouste engine, 530 horse power.

Alouette II